SHARKS

ERIK D. STOOPS & SHERRIE STOOPS

Sterling Publishing Co., Inc. New York

Library of Congress Cataloging-in-Publication Data

Stoops, Erik D., 1966–
    Sharks / Erik Stoops & Sherrie Stoops.
      p. cm.
    Includes index.
    ISBN 0-8069-0374-0
    1. Sharks—Juvenile literature. [1. Sharks.] I. Stoops,
Sherrie. II. Title.   105
    QL638.9.S846   1994
    597′.31—dc20
                                          93-43336
                                              CIP
                                              AC

Cover photo: Blue Shark by Michael Nolan

Design by Judy Morgan

10 9 8 7 6 5 4 3 2 1

First paperback edition published in 1995 by
Sterling Publishing Company, Inc.
387 Park Avenue South, New York, N.Y. 10016
© 1994 by Erik D. Stoops & Sherrie Stoops
Distributed in Canada by Sterling Publishing
℅ Canadian Manda Group, One Atlantic Avenue, Suite 105
Toronto, Ontario, Canada M6K 3E7
Distributed in Great Britain and Europe by Cassell PLC
Wellington House, 125 Strand, London WC2R 0BB, England
Distributed in Australia by Capricorn Link (Australia) Pty Ltd.
P.O. Box 6651, Baulkham Hills, Business Centre, NSW 2153, Australia
Printed and bound in Hong Kong
All rights reserved

Sterling ISBN 0-8069-0374-0 Trade
              0-8069-0373-2 Paper

CONTENTS

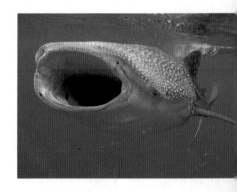

Scalloped Hammerhead
Sharks have sometimes been
seen swimming in large
numbers. This is certainly an
unusual sight for many divers
and scientists.

HOW SHARKS LIVE

Sharks, just like people, come in all shapes and sizes. They live in different waters all over the world. Are all of them dangerous? Are some of them gentle? How do they live? These are just a few of the questions that get asked all the time. Read on and get some answers.

By Wesley R. Strong

By Tom Campbell

▲Bonnethead Sharks are named for their hat-shaped heads.

By Doug Perrine

▲The Tiger Shark got its name from the faint brown stripes that go up and down its sides.

What are sharks?

Sharks are fishes that have skeletons made of cartilage instead of bones. Cartilage is a tough, flexible material that is also found in people's joints. It's in knees, elbows, shoulders and even on the end of our nose. Most other fishes have skeletons made of bones.

What do sharks look like?

Sharks generally have stream-lined bodies, fins and gills. But there are many types of sharks and they are vastly different in size, shape, color and habits.

How big do sharks get?

Sharks range in size from the Dwarf Shark, which would fit in your hand, to the giant Whale Shark, which can grow up to 45 feet (14m) long.

Where do sharks live?

Sharks are found mostly in salt water—in all oceans, from shallow waters near the shore and coral reefs to the open ocean and the bottom of the sea. Some are also found in freshwater lakes and rivers.

By Wesley R. Strong

▲The Whitetip Reef Shark fits the description of the "typical" shark.

▶The Grey Reef Shark is often seen in tropical reefs and lagoons, but it is also comfortable in deeper water.

By Wesley R. Strong

Do sharks like warm or cold water?

Basically, each species likes different temperatures. Tropical species are found in water that is warmer than 70°F (21°C). Temperate species are found where the water is from 50° to 69°F (10° to 20°C). Cold water sharks live where the temperature is between 33° and 50°F (0.6° and 10°C). Some shark species can be found in all three.

How many different kinds of sharks are there?

Scientists know about 360 different species, but this number is increasing as more species are discovered.

What is the most well known shark?

The best known shark of all is the Great White. A powerful swimmer, with a mouthful of huge teeth, it is one of the largest hunters.

▼ **The Great White was the shark species portrayed in the film *Jaws*.**

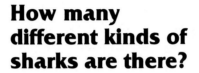

▲ **The Scalloped Hammerhead is different from many other species of shark because its head is actually shaped like a hammer! Some scientists think the head acts like an extra fin.**

By Doug Perrine

By James D. Wat

What is the most common shark?

Scientist say there are more Spiny Dogfish than any other kind of shark. It is found in temperate and cold waters worldwide.

▶**Spiny Dogfish swim in large groups or schools. Not many kinds of sharks do. Schools of Spiny Dogfish number in the thousands.**

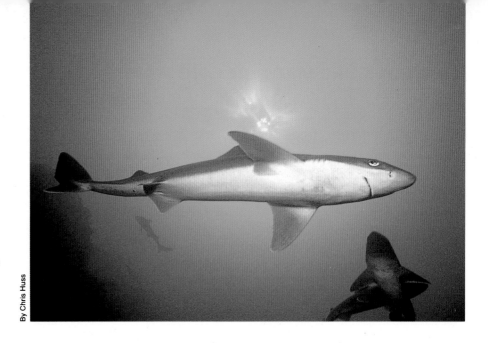

By Chris Huss

By Bruce Rasner

▲**A gentle giant of the sea, the largest Megamouth found so far measured 16 feet (4.9m) long.**

▶**A diver comes face to face with the first Megamouth to be photographed alive.**

What is the rarest shark?

The rarest shark known is the Megamouth. It is seldom seen because it spends much of its time deep in the ocean. To date, only six of these sharks have been seen. They were found off the coasts of Hawaii, California, Australia and Japan.

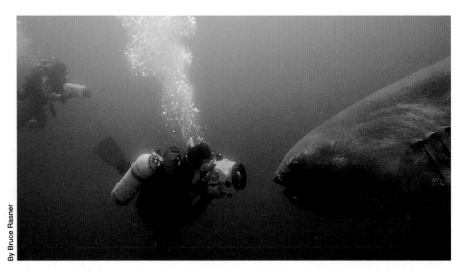

By Bruce Rasner

What is the largest shark?

The Whale Shark is the largest fish in the world. It can grow to a length of 45 feet (14m)! That's bigger than a school bus! It can weigh 15 tons or more.

▶ **Despite its great size, the Whale Shark eats only tiny shrimp and fish.**

By Norbert Wu

By Jeffrey L. Martin

What is the smallest shark?

The smallest shark in the world is probably the Dwarf Shark. It can reach a total length of 9.8 inches (25cm). Mature specimens that measure less than six inches (15cm) have been found! Most of them live in deep oceans—3,000 feet (900m) or deeper.

What is the strangest-looking shark?

The Goblin shark has a flat pointy snout that hangs out over its head. It looks as if it lived during the Cretaceous period (the last part of the Age of the Dinosaurs). It's probably the strangest-looking.

▲ **Scientists thought the Goblin Shark was long extinct until a four-foot (1.2m) specimen was pulled from the Sea of Japan in the late 1800s.**

9

By Doug Perrine

By James D. Watt

▲Divers often use large pieces of bait to attract Great White Sharks.

What other sharks attack humans?

Other dangerous sharks include the fast-swimming Mako, the Oceanic Whitetip Shark, the Tiger Shark and the Great Hammerhead Shark.

What is a "rogue" shark?

Lame or sick sharks cannot swim as fast as healthy ones and have a hard time capturing their natural prey. That's why they sometimes swim into waters that they would not normally visit—to find easier prey to catch. These sharks, known as "rogues," have an easy time surprising or outrunning humans.

What is the most dangerous shark?

▲The Bull Shark is probably the most dangerous shark you're likely to meet, because it is frequently found in warm, shallow water.

Because of its large size and huge, razor-sharp teeth, the Great White is the shark most people think of as the most dangerous. Fortunately, it doesn't normally swim in shallow waters where people swim. It is also uncommon, so the chances of meeting one are slim.

Are all sharks dangerous to people?

No, most sharks are harmless to people. But nearly any wild animal may attack if threatened or provoked.

By Wesley R. Strong

By Norbert Wu

▲The Blue Shark is normally harmless to divers, but it can be provoked. Here divers are experimenting with steel-mesh suits for possible protection against shark attack.

◄The Grey Nurse is large and looks scary, but it shies away from humans and lives on a diet of fish.

By Doug Perrine

▲The Nurse Shark is peaceful, but it has been responsible for many attacks in self-defense when divers pull its tail.

Are any sharks friendly to humans?

Not exactly, but some species seem to view humans as harmless. Whale Sharks are large enough to swallow humans whole, but they feed only on plankton and small fish. These gentle giants have allowed divers to ride on their back and dorsal fins.

By Tom Campbell

▲The Basking Shark can grow longer than 25 feet (8m), but it has only tiny teeth like the Whale Shark. It is not a danger to humans.

How long do sharks live?

This is still something of a mystery. Some sharks have been known to live 75 years or more. The Spiny Dogfish can live up to 100 years, which might make it one of the longest-lived sharks. But most sharks have unknown life spans.

When did the first sharks live?

The earliest known sharks, the *cladodonts* (CLAD-o-dahnts), lived about 370 million years ago. This was before the Age of the Dinosaurs.

▲The Grey Nurse Shark is a large animal that can live for at least 20 years.

By Doug Perrine

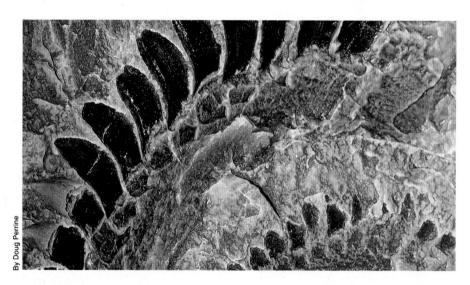

By Doug Perrine

By Doug Perrine

◄*Cladoselache* (clad-o-suh-LOCH-y), a cladodont shark, was an ancestor of modern sharks.

▲*Helicoprion* (hel-AKO-PRY-on) was a primitive shark that lived 300 million years ago. Its teeth were very different from sharks' teeth today. It had rows of teeth that were rolled up in its gums.

► This woman is standing in the reconstructed jaws of the prehistoric giant, *Carcharodon megalodon*.

What is the largest shark fossil ever found?

The *Carcharodon megalodon* (kar-kare-OH-don meg-a-LO-don) is the largest shark fossil found so far. Its name means "rough tooth–huge tooth." The only parts of this huge shark that were ever found were its teeth and some pieces of backbone.

► Here is what the *Carcharodon megalodon* may have looked like. Notice its size compared to the diver.

By Doug Perrine

By Jeffrey L. Martin

13

► The giant Manta Ray can measure up to 20 feet (6m) across! It swims in the open ocean.

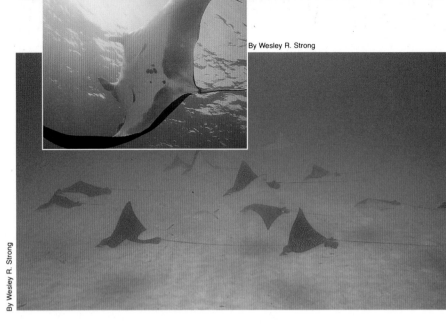
By Wesley R. Strong

By Wesley R. Strong

Do sharks have any relatives?

Yes. Sharks are closely related to rays and skates. They are also related to strange-looking fish called chimaeras (ki-MEER-az) or ratfishes. Sharks, rays, skates and chimaeras all have skeletons made of cartilage.

▲ This school of Eagle Rays has gathered in the warm waters of the Bahamas.

What are chimaeras like?

These primitive fish have rabbit-like noses and long, thin tails. Most chimaeras also have very long spines (spikes) in their dorsal fins (the fins on their back). They usually live in very deep water and are rarely seen by humans.

▼ The Spotted Eagle Ray got its name from the beautiful spots on its back. It spends most of its life gliding through the water.

By David B. Fleetham

▲ The chimaera or ratfish got its name from its rat-like tail.

14

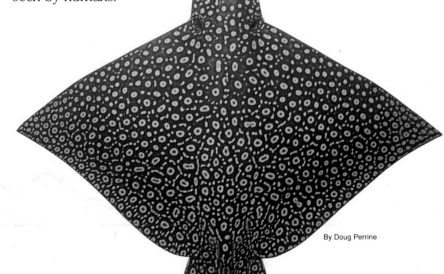
By Doug Perrine

◄Like most rays, Southern Stingrays lie hidden in the sand on the ocean floor. Stingrays get their name from the poisonous stinging spines on their tails. They use them for self-defense.

◄This beautiful manta is the largest ray. It makes spectacular leaps out of the water.

►The Guitarfish is a ray, but it swims like a shark, with a side-to-side motion of its tail.

►The Sawfish, another shark relative, has a long snout edged with sharp denticles, tooth-like scales that it uses to slash prey fish.

►The Angel Shark, named for its wing-like fins, has a flat body like a ray, but is considered a shark because its fins come out of its chest instead of its head. Some scientists say it is a shark on its way to becoming a ray.

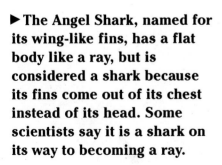

15

Do sharks have friends?

Not really, but several species of fish often swim with them. Pilot fish, for example, feed on small scraps of food left by the sharks. They also hang around the shark in order to be protected from their enemies.

By Wesley R. Strong

By Wesley R. Strong

Are any fish helpful to sharks?

Remoras and sharksuckers, slim-bodied fish with flat heads, eat the parasites that attach themselves to sharks. Remoras swim with sharks, but also sometimes attach themselves to sharks, using a sucker disc they have on their head. Sharks seem to know that remoras are performing a service and do not try to eat them.

16

◄If you look closely, you will see a remora attached to the underside of this Blue Shark.

▼This Lemon Shark is accompanied by a sharksucker. This creature eats parasites off the shark's skin, gills, and even from inside its mouth.

▲This Blue Shark is accompanied by a group of jack mackerels, which are probably waiting for food scraps from the shark's next meal.

By Doug Perrine

What species travels farthest?

Blue Sharks are thought to migrate the farthest of all sharks. Specimens caught and tagged off the east coast of the U.S. have been recovered over 3,500 miles (5,600km) away near Brazil and the west coast of Africa. Bull Sharks have been found over 2,300 miles (3,680km) from the sea in the Amazon River in South America.

What do sharks die of?

Sharks are killed by people and by underwater hunters, such as barracudas, groupers, swordfish and killer whales. Sharks also get diseases and infections. Their immune system can be weakened by pollution and parasites. They can choke to death on items that are too large to swallow. Some sharks die of suffocation if their forward motion is stopped. Thousands die each year in gill nets for this reason. When they are caught and pulled from the water, their skeletons cannot support their weight. Their organs get damaged and they bleed to death. Also, many sharks die from being struck by boats.

By Wesley R. Strong

By Wesley R. Strong

▲This is a school of Scalloped Hammerhead Sharks. Sharks don't usually travel in schools or groups, but they do gather for migration, mating and feeding.

◄This Nurse Shark is caught in a piece of loose fishing line that is cutting into its head. Fishing line is dangerous to all sea animals.

This Oceanic Whitetip Shark is an excellent hunter. Its large muscular body makes it a powerful swimmer.

THE SHARK'S BODY

Sharks' bodies may be flat or torpedo-shaped. They may be blue, white, grey, tan, brown, black, greenish, or even purplish. There are scary-looking species, such as the ghostly-looking Goblin Shark. There are species that look like something out of a science fiction movie, like the Hammerhead Shark. Some features of the shark's anatomy are different from all other animals. But however they look, their bodies have evolved to perfectly suit the environment in which they live.

▶ **Sharks' bodies are generally streamlined. This helps them to be great swimmers and hunters. The Blue Shark is a good example of this.**

Are sharks fishes or mammals?

Sharks are fishes. They have paired fins, gills and a heart with two chambers in it. Mammals, on the other hand, have hair, lungs and a four-chambered heart. Sharks resemble dolphins and whales, which are mammals, but are not related to them.

By Mark Conlin

By Doug Perrine

▶ **Dolphins and sharks share a streamlined body shape that makes swimming easier. This spotted dolphin has a scar on its side from a shark bite.**

By James D. Watt

19

Do sharks ever get cold?

No one knows what sensations a shark feels, but many species seem perfectly comfortable in nearly freezing water.

Do sharks have skin or scales?

The shark's skin is covered by denticles, tooth-like scales that are usually small and act like armor, protecting the body against rough objects. Because of tiny bumps and ridges on each scale, shark skin feels rough, like sandpaper.

Are sharks cold-blooded?

Most sharks are completely cold-blooded. This means they cannot create their own body heat, and so they take on the temperature of the water around them. Fast-swimming sharks such as Whites, Makos and Porbeagles can save heat built up by their muscles. They have special blood vessels called the retia (REE-sha) that carry this heat and keep their temperature a few degrees higher than the water.

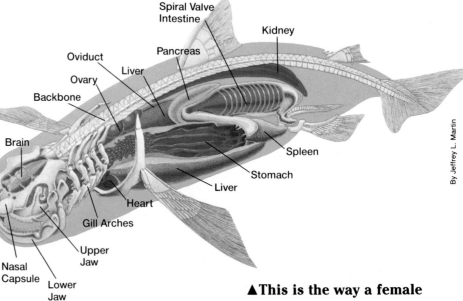

Spiral Valve Intestine
Kidney
Oviduct
Pancreas
Liver
Ovary
Backbone
Brain
Spleen
Stomach
Liver
Skull
Heart
Gill Arches
Upper Jaw
Nasal Capsule
Lower Jaw

By Jeffrey L. Martin

By Doug Perrine

◄If you look closely, you can see the denticles on this Nurse Shark.

▲This is the way a female Spiny Dogfish looks on the inside. These sharks are among the most studied and best understood of all sharks, because there are so many of them.

How powerful is a shark's jaw?

Scientists have developed a shark-bite meter that helps answer this question. One study showed that the jaws of a Dusky Shark apply the pressure of about 18 tons per square inch on its victim when it bites. This is like the weight of ten cars!

▶ **This Tiger, like most sharks, has five pairs of gills.**

▼ **The Sixgill Shark is one of the few species that possess six pairs of gills. One species has seven.**

By David B. Fleetham

How do sharks breathe?

They generally swim with their mouths open, so that water passes over their gills and out through their gill slits. Water contains dissolved oxygen, which sharks need in order to live. Their gills absorb the oxygen from the water and transfer it into the bloodstream. Gills also get rid of carbon dioxide, a waste product of breathing.

By Doug Perrine

What is a gill raker?

Gill rakers keep food particles from slipping out through the shark's gill slits. They work like a kitchen strainer that drains noodles after they are cooked.

▶ **Some sharks' gill rakers look like feathers.**

By Doug Perrine

What are the holes on the sides of the shark's head?

They are the spiracle, which means "air holes" in Latin. The spiracle draws water past the gills, so they don't get clogged up with sand. The spiracle evolved to become the ear canal in many land animals, including humans.

How does a shark digest its food?

After food is broken down in the shark's stomach, it travels through a special "spiral valve." It is a fold of tissue that winds down inside the shark's intestine. It increases the size of the intestine so that the shark can absorb more digested food. The spiral valve looks like a spiral staircase. After the food moves through the spiral valve, the nutrients are absorbed into the blood. What's left passes through the colon and out of the shark's body.

What is the largest organ in a shark's body?

The liver makes up five to 25 percent of the shark's total body weight. Because the liver is rich in oil, it is lighter than water. This helps the shark float, which makes swimming easier.

Does a shark have a nose?

The nose of the shark is called its snout. It has two "nares" (nostrils) for smelling things—but not for breathing. That's because the nares don't connect with the shark's throat the way a human nose does.

By Doug Perrine

▲This close-up of the snout of a Tiger Shark shows its nares.

By Doug Perrine

Does a shark have a tongue?

Yes, but not all sharks can move their tongue.

Do sharks smile?

They have a sort of grin, but it is not an expression of emotion. Small folds, called labial furrows, in the corners of a shark's mouth, are responsible for that "smile." No one knows what else the labial furrows do.

▲You can easily see the labial furrows on this Tiger Shark.

23

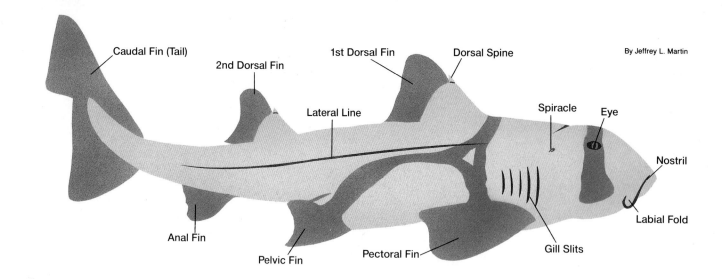

By Jeffrey L. Martin

Caudal Fin (Tail)

2nd Dorsal Fin

1st Dorsal Fin

Dorsal Spine

Lateral Line

Spiracle

Eye

Nostril

Labial Fold

Anal Fin

Pelvic Fin

Pectoral Fin

Gill Slits

▲This drawing of the Horn Shark (also known as the Port Jackson Shark) shows all its outer parts.

◄The Nurse Shark is one of the few species that has a second dorsal fin that is nearly as large as the first.

Where are a shark's fins?

Most sharks have five types of fins:

1. Located at the base of the gills is a pair of fins that steer and lift the shark as it swims. There is one on each side. They are called the pectoral fins.

2. A large single fin on its back keeps the shark from rolling while it steers. Most sharks have a second smaller fin behind it on their back that works in the same way. These are called the dorsal fins.

3. Another pair flank the vent (where wastes are eliminated). They steady the shark while it swims. These are called the pelvic fins.

4. The shark has one small fin between the pelvic fins and

24

By Doug Perrine

the tail, or caudal, fin. This also keeps the shark from rolling over while it swims. It is called the anal fin.

5. The caudal, or tail, fin provides most of the force for swimming.

▲ The Lemon Shark has a dorsal fin that sticks out of the water when it is swimming just below the surface. This is what people see when they spot a shark in the water. Dolphin fins look very similar.

By Norbert Wu

What is a caudal keel?

The caudal keel is a stiff, flat horizontal ridge found at the base of the tail of some shark species. It supports the shark's tail. Slow but powerful swimmers, such as Basking Sharks, as well as some fast swimmers, have a caudal keel.

▲Most "typical" sharks have a caudal keel. You can see it easily on this Shortfin Mako.

How do sharks swim?

Sharks swim by moving their tail from side to side. This drives the shark forward. Most sharks swim with a slinky movement, but the White Shark, Mako and Porbeagle swim stiffly, like the tuna and swordfish.

By Len Tillim

◄ **This Shortfin Mako is probably one of the fastest sharks. It has to be fast to catch its favorite food— mackerel and tuna.**

► **This spotted Wobbegong is a slow swimmer that usually hides on the bottom of the ocean and waits to grab prey animals that come close.**

By Doug Perrine

▼ **You can see the parasites on the mouth of this Scalloped Hammerhead Shark.**

By Doug Perrine

Do sharks get sick?

Yes. Sharks have been found with internal parasites such as tapeworms and roundworms, and with external parasites like copepods (small relatives of the crab).

Parasites feed on the shark's blood or its digested food and can weaken the shark. Some sharks get liver disease and tumors. Some suffer from skin cuts and bruises.

27

This Tiger Shark is ripping chunks from a dead Humpback Whale.

EATING HABITS

What and how sharks eat depends on where and how they live. Some are filter feeders, sweeping up plankton with their huge mouths.

Some are fast swimmers that catch fish with their sharp, pointed teeth. Still others search the coastline for seals, dolphins and seabirds.

Many are bottom-dwellers that feed on crabs and shellfish in the ocean. All eat other animals.

Are sharks picky eaters?

Sharks will eat what they can, when they can. However, each species has a diet that it prefers. Some sharks will eat just about anything.

▶ **Scientists and photographers use mackerel, a favorite of the Blue Shark, to attract and study it.**

By Michael Nolan

What do sharks usually eat?

Most sharks eat animals smaller than themselves. That ranges from clams, shrimp, squid and fish to sea turtles and seabirds. Some sharks eat large mammals, such as sea lions, dolphins and even dead or dying whales. Some eat only plankton, tiny drifting animals and plants.

Do sharks eat other sharks?

Yes, Bull Sharks, Tigers and Great Whites eat other sharks. The Shortfin Mako has also been known to eat Blue Sharks, Grey Sharks and Hammerhead Sharks. Nurse Sharks eat other Nurse Sharks, too.

By Mark Conlin

By Michael Nolan

▲The sea lion swims in the same area as the Blue Shark. Although the sea lion is too big for the Blue Shark to eat, it is perfect prey for the Great White.

Do sharks eat dead animals?

Sharks normally will not eat dead animals, especially if they are decaying. But they will eat sick or weak animals. Many dead whales have been found partially eaten by sharks.

▲The Blue Shark eats mackerels whole, but will tear chunks of flesh from larger prey when it gets the chance.

Do sharks eat anything else?

Some unusual items found in the stomachs of Tiger Sharks include tires, sacks of nails, spools of wire, canned fish, wristwatches, nuts and bolts and even paint cans!

▶ **The Tiger Shark eats reptiles, mammals, birds, fish and a variety of man-made objects.**

By Doug Perrine

By Michael Conlin

▲ **The Blue Shark has been observed swimming through huge schools of krill and eating large numbers of them.**

How do sharks eat?

Some sharks will swallow their prey, usually small fishes, whole. Others will bite and tear large chunks out of their prey. Still others will crush the shells of crabs or clams. Some sharks swim with their mouths open and swallow tons of tiny sea creatures. This is called "filter feeding."

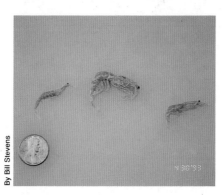

By Bill Stevens

◀ **These tiny shrimps are called "krill." Filter feeders, such as Whale Sharks and Basking Sharks, as well as large whales, eat them by the ton.**

31

Can sharks taste their food?

Yes, but unlike humans, who have taste buds only on their tongues, sharks also have taste buds in their throats and all through their mouths.

Do sharks chew their food?

Because most sharks have knife-like teeth, they cannot use them for chewing. They don't have molars and their jaws are not designed for grinding food.

What do sharks' teeth look like?

There are almost as many kinds of sharks' teeth as there are sharks! The Great White Shark's teeth are broad triangles that can tear meat easily. The Basking Shark is nearly toothless, since it is a filter feeder.

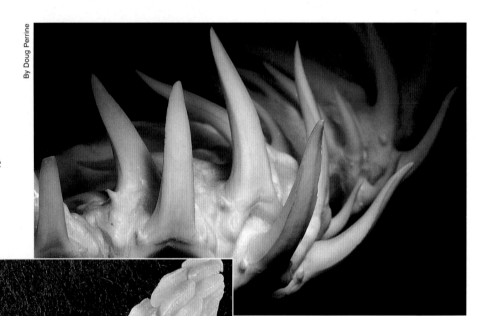

By Doug Perrine

By Doug Perrine

▲The shape of a tooth can tell you a lot about a shark's diet. Sharp, curved teeth help the Shortfin Mako grasp, hold fast and swallow slippery fish.

◄The Horn Shark uses its flat jaws for crushing shellfish that it likes to eat.

Do sharks ever lose their teeth?

Yes, they lose many thousands of teeth in a lifetime. Their teeth either fall out or are pushed out. They also lose teeth while feeding. But about every two weeks sharks get a new set of teeth. The back rows of teeth move forward to replace the lost ones. Sharks' teeth are not planted in sockets in their jawbones, as human teeth are. They are set loosely in the top layer of skin inside their mouths.

How many teeth does a shark have?

Many sharks have five to ten rows of teeth in their mouths, but most of these are replacement rows. They normally use only two to three rows at a time.

What is a shark's tooth made of?

A shark's tooth has an inner bony layer that contains a nerve and blood vessels. This layer is covered by an outer layer of enamel that makes the tooth very hard and durable.

▼Shark jaws are often bought as "conversation pieces." This is a sad way to talk about sharks. These jaws used to belong to a Mako.

▲These are the replacement teeth on the inside of a Tiger Shark's jaw. Tiger Shark teeth are perfect for tearing and cutting.

You can see the enamel ▲ that protects the tooth of a Great White Shark.

33

Do most sharks have big teeth?

No, the Basking Shark has very small, almost invisible teeth. So do other filter feeders. Big teeth would be of no use to them.

How does a shark capture its food?

Most sharks circle very cautiously. Then they bump their prey to make sure it won't fight back. A violent reaction will send the sharks darting off, but then they will start the process all over again. Some lie in wait for their prey to swim by.

Does a shark eat all the time?

No, most sharks can go months between meals. The shark's liver, with lots of oil and fat in it, helps the shark go without food for a long period of time after a good meal.

Do sharks ever eat too much?

Sharks sometimes gorge themselves (eat more food than they need), but they will then wait a longer time before their next meal. Usually sharks only eat as much as they need to survive.

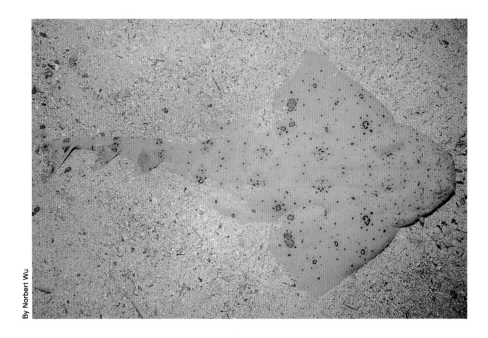

By Norbert Wu

▲This Angel Shark is lying hidden on the ocean floor, waiting to capture its prey— crabs, shrimp and lobsters.

By Doug Perrine

▲The Chain Dogfish is a very small species—about 18 inches (45cm) long, so it doesn't need as much food as larger sharks.

Can a shark get fat?

If sharks were to get fat, it would be difficult for them to catch their prey. Most sharks have a high activity level that prevents them from getting fat. Sharks normally eat right naturally.

What is a feeding frenzy?

Sharks generally like to swim alone. But if there is easy prey in the area, a group of them may gather. Sometimes the excitement of the competition causes the sharks to feed too quickly. Their senses become confused and they bite anything that gets in their way.

By Michael Nolan

▲Divers create a feeding frenzy by scattering bait in the water.

▼During a feeding frenzy, sharks such as these Blues will eat anything, including each other!

By Michael Nolan

How big can a shark's mouth get?

The mouth of the Whale Shark may be over four feet (1.2m) wide!

▲The Whale Shark may have a huge mouth, but this huge animal is not interested in eating anything bigger than a small fish. It will spit out any large object.

How big a thing can sharks swallow?

There are reports of 15-foot (4.5m) White Sharks found with whole adult dolphins and sea lions in their stomachs. Sharks measuring six to seven feet (2m) have also been found. Some people believe that Jonah in the Bible was swallowed by a shark, not a whale. Sharks are more likely to swallow people than whales are.

Do sharks drink water?

Sharks get all the liquid they need from the food they eat. They also naturally swallow water with their food.

▲ The Great White Shark can be extremely dangerous when in the presence of bait.

Do sharks throw up?

Sometimes hard-to-digest objects, like turtle shells, are thrown up by sharks. The Lemon Shark has been observed vomiting in a very different way. When its stomach is upset, this shark "throws up" its entire stomach! Then it shakes and rinses out its stomach and swallows it back into place.

▲ The Sandbar Shark may swallow a small sea turtle by mistake and throw it up. Then, often, the little turtle just swims away.

This Great White Shark has checked out its prey by sound, scent, sight, electrical signal and touch. Now its jaws are open wide to bite its prey and taste-test it.

THE SHARK'S SENSES

All the shark's senses are vital to its survival. Scientists believe that a shark relies on different senses at different distances. Since sound travels much farther and five times faster in water than in air, a shark will most likely hear its prey first. As it investigates, the shark may next pick up a scent, perhaps of blood, and follow it to its source. When it gets within visual range, it circles cautiously and then approaches, picking up weak electrical signals from its prey. It bumps the prey and then strikes. If the prey tastes right, the shark will keep feeding.

By Doug Perrine

By James D. Watt

◄ **This Caribbean Reef Shark has found some bait and is preparing to strike.**

How does a shark hear?

Sound travels through water the way ripples do when you throw a pebble into a pond. These ripples are called pressure waves. The canals and chambers in each inner ear detect these waves. Scientists are still trying to discover new ways in which sharks hear sound.

Do sharks have ears?

While a shark doesn't have ears on the outside like humans, it does have inner ears. They receive sound waves and help the shark keep its balance in the water. Three canals filled with liquid plus large and small chambers in each ear tell the shark's brain about its speed in the water.

What kinds of sounds can sharks hear?

Scientific experiments show that sharks can hear a wide range of sounds, but they are attracted mostly by the low-pitched ones. They especially respond to bursts of sound, the type of noise an injured fish makes. Unfortunately, it is also the same sound healthy humans make when they are playing in the water. At close range, the shark's "lateral line" can also sense these vibrations.

What is the "lateral line"?

Lying just below the shark's skin, the lateral line reaches from the tail to the head on each side of the body. Inside it are canals filled with fluid and tiny "hair cells" that are triggered by vibrations in the water. They help the shark keep its balance and detect sound.

◄ **The Nurse Shark, because it is so common, is often tested by scientists who are studying the hearing of sharks, and their other senses.**

▲ **The lateral line is visible on the side of this Lemon Shark.**

How does the lateral line work?

Pressure waves vibrate the liquid in the lateral canal. These waves could be caused by a fish moving nearby or by the shark swimming close to a reef. The lateral line alerts the shark so it can catch the fish or avoid the reef, even in total darkness. This is very important to a species of shark that hunts by night.

How does a shark smell things?

The shark's powerful sense of smell can even detect chemicals in the water—just as humans can often smell airborne chemicals. As we already saw, the shark's nose doesn't connect with its throat, but it does have nostrils (nares) that are packed with cells that detect odors.

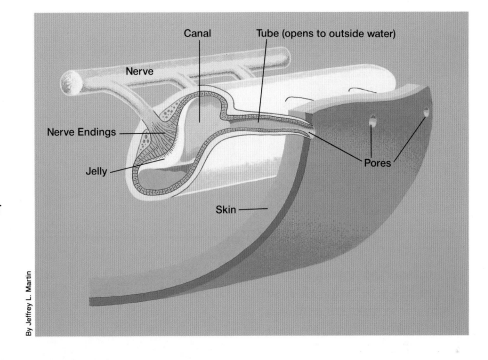

By Jeffrey L. Martin

▲ This drawing shows how the lateral line looks from the inside. The illustration is much larger than the lateral line of a real shark.

▼ The Sharpnose Shark often uses its snout to smell out and then actually reach into rock crevices to get at hidden food on the ocean floor.

By Doug Perrine

How does a shark use its sense of smell?

A shark picks up the scent of blood or other body fluids. Its sense of smell is so sensitive that it can detect one part of blood in many millions of parts of water. That is enough to lead it to its prey.

Do sharks make sounds?

No, the shark is a fish, one of the few animals that do not have vocal chords. It has no way to utter a sound in the water.

Can sharks see color?

Most scientists think sharks can see some color. We know the Lemon Shark can tell the difference between red and white. But it is hard to know whether red looks red or grey to a Lemon Shark.

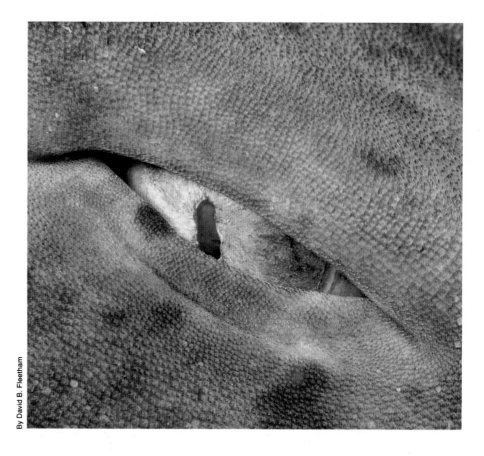

By David B. Fleetham

Are a shark's eyes different from other fishes'?

The color part (the iris) of the shark's eye can open and close to let more or less light get to the retina. Bony fishes can't do that. The opening in the iris is called the pupil. In most sharks it is a cat-like slit.

▲ The Swell Shark is a member of the Catshark family, which is named for its cat-like eyes.

42

By Doug Perrine

◀The Caribbean Reef Shark, like many other sharks and rays, can see well enough to tell the difference between objects and their watery background.

Do sharks have eyelids?

Most sharks have upper and lower eyelids that don't move. But some sharks have a thick, fleshy third eyelid at the bottom of the eye. It can cover the eye completely and protect it during feeding. It is called the "nictitating membrane."

Do sharks see clearly?

Scientists aren't sure how clearly different shark species can focus. They believe that species who live in the open ocean are farsighted and reef dwellers are nearsighted.

How do sharks see in the dark?

Like many other animals that hunt at night, a shark's eyes have a mirror-like layer in the back called the tapetum. It helps the shark see in dim light. Sharks possess dark-colored cells that cover and uncover the tapetum, when the light gets too bright or too dim. They work something like window curtains.

By Norbert Wu

▲You can see the nictitating membrane covering the eye of this Blue Shark as it swims.

43

How does a shark sense electricity?

All living things produce small amounts of electricity just by moving. Sharks can detect this electricity using electro-receptors called the "ampullae (am-POOL-ee) of Lorenzini."

What are the ampullae of Lorenzini?

They are small pits on the shark's head and snout, filled with a sort of clear jelly. Using signals from these pits, a shark can find its prey even if it is completely buried in sand or mud. The pits may also act as a compass for the shark.

▼ **A highly magnified view of the ampullae of Lorenzini and the shark's facial nerves.**

By James D. Watt

▲**You can see the ampullae of Lorenzini on this Great White Shark. They are the dark spots on its snout.**

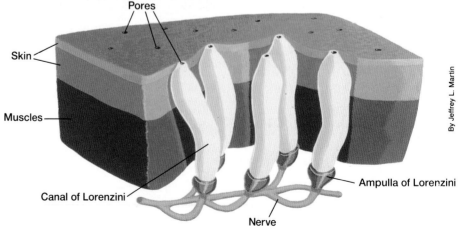

Pores

Skin

Muscles

Canal of Lorenzini

Ampulla of Lorenzini

Nerve

By Jeffrey L. Martin

44

What are barbels?

Barbels are fleshy feelers at the front or sides of the mouths of some shark species. Scientists believe sharks use them to feel around in the sand for prey.

▼ **This Tawny Nurse Shark shows its barbels, which look like sharp teeth.**

By Mark Strickland

Are sharks smart?

Yes, experiments show that they can recognize and remember patterns and shapes. Lemon Sharks have been taught to ring bells, press targets and even swim through mazes to receive rewards of food.

Can a shark feel pain?

No one really knows. During feeding frenzies, sharks that are seriously injured continue feeding. They seem to be completely unaware that they are hurt! Maybe the excitement keeps them from noticing. But sharks do have nerves, so they probably feel pain.

Are sharks' brains anything like ours?

They have most of the same major parts, but sharks have an important part that humans don't have—a "forebrain" that includes its olfactory bulbs (sense of smell). The shark's brain is fairly small compared to its body.

The Swell Shark can swallow water to make its body much larger. It can wedge itself between rocks so that its enemies can't pull it out.

SELF-DEFENSE

Like all other animals, the shark has ways of protecting itself from its enemies. Predators usually think very carefully before attacking a shark, with its mouth full of sharp teeth and its rough skin that can scrape an attacker.

Who are the shark's natural enemies?

Sometimes larger sharks are caught with smaller sharks inside their bellies. Killer whales also eat sharks, but the enemies that kill the most sharks are humans. People kill sharks for food and sport. Thousands of sharks suffocate in gill nets each year.

What is a gill net?

Fishermen use huge nets—gill nets—to catch large numbers of fish. Sea mammals and sharks are often caught in these nets, where they get tangled up and finally drown.

Can a shark drown?

Yes! Even though they live underwater, sharks can and do drown when water does not run freely over their gills. Sometimes they may get injured so badly that they cannot swim and then they drown.

▼ **The Thresher Shark is sometimes caught with the fishhook stuck in its tail instead of its mouth. Some scientists think it is trying to stun the bait fish and ends up getting caught by the tail.**

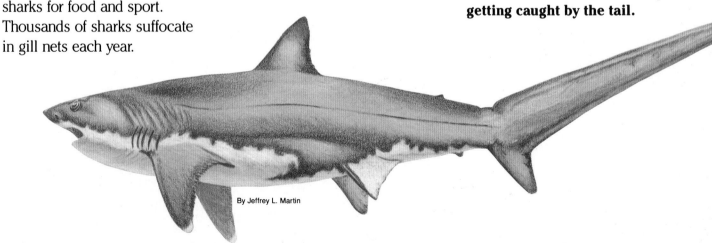

By Jeffrey L. Martin

By Norbert Wu

What protects sharks from attacks by other animals?

Denticles, made out of the same material as teeth, are found all over the skin of most sharks. Generally, denticles are very small, coming to a sharp point and facing towards the tail. The Bramble Shark has such large, thorn-like denticles, though, that if a larger shark tries to eat a Bramble Shark, its denticles make the attacker throw up.

Does a shark's color protect it?

Yes, most sharks are dark grey or blue on their backs, with a lighter color on their bellies. This pattern is called "counter-shading." It helps to hide the shark from its prey or predators. Bottom-dwelling sharks who live near the coast are often speckled or banded to blend in with the rocks and reefs.

▶ **As you can see, the colors of this Ornate Wobbegong camouflage it well.**

▶ **This Silky Shark looks dark from above and light from below, just like the ocean. This counter-shading helps it blend in with its surroundings.**

By Wesley R. Strong

By Doug Perrine

What about bright-colored sharks?

Some sharks, such as Leopard Sharks, Bamboo Sharks and Chain Catsharks, have striking markings with contrasting bands, spots or patterns. Surprisingly, this bold coloring camouflages these sharks by breaking up the outline of their bodies.

By Mark Conlin

By Mark Conlin

▲The Bamboo Shark can climb up reef rocks and even live out of the water for hours. In this way it can catch its prey and avoid its enemies. When it is in the water, its outline is disguised by its colorful markings.

◀The Leopard Shark's bold markings startle its enemies as it darts out from coral reef heads—and give it time to escape.

Are any sharks poisonous?

The meat of the Greenland Shark is poisonous if eaten by people, though it can be prepared so that it is edible. Spiny Dogfish and some other sharks have fin spines that can be painful to the touch, but are not poisonous. Being stung by the tail spines of a stingray can be extremely painful and sometimes deadly.

How do sharks sleep?

Some sharks need to keep swimming in order to stay alive. They seem to swim in their sleep. Bottom-dwelling sharks just slip into a dormant or inactive state, which may not be true sleep.

▶The Nurse Shark takes short rests on the bottom of the ocean during the day and becomes active at night.

By Doug Perrine

▲This Caribbean Reef Shark is resting on the bottom of the ocean in a dormant state.

By Doug Perrine

50

Do all sharks rest during the day?

No, some sharks are active only during the day, some only during the night.

Do sharks close their eyes while sleeping?

No, sharks with movable eyelids (nictitating membranes) use them only to protect their eyes from hard or sharp objects or while feeding.

By Wesley R. Strong

By Doug Perrine

▲Some sharks, such as this Nurse Shark, can pump water over their gills so that they don't need to swim constantly and can "sleep."

◄The Caribbean Reef Shark can be aggressive. It is known as a "man-biter," but not a "man-eater."

This Swell Shark is getting ready to emerge from its egg case.

SHARK REPRODUCTION

The shark is different from many other animals in that some species lay eggs while others give live birth. All sharks fertilize their eggs inside their bodies. They produce well-developed young that can fend for themselves and usually survive. Most other fishes fertilize their eggs outside their bodies. There is still much to learn about shark reproduction, because these animals are so difficult to study.

What does "fertilize" mean?

An egg cell is fertilized when a male's sperm cell meets it and creates a complete cell that can develop into an embryo—and eventually a baby shark.

How do you tell a male from a female shark?

The male has a clasper on each of its two pelvic fins, and you can easily see them. The female has no claspers. To see other differences, you would have to dissect the sharks.

By Doug Perrine

▲ **This Bull Shark's claspers can be seen extending from its pelvic fins. They are white.**

By Mark Conlin

What are claspers?

Claspers are the male shark's external reproductive organs. They are like tubes that come out of its pelvic fins.

How do sharks attract each other?

Only a few shark species have been observed courting. Some scientists believe that females may give off chemical signals, as well as visual ones, to attract the male. Female Reef Sharks have been seen performing a swimming ritual with slightly lifted tails. Males were seen swimming very closely behind them. In other species, it's more a question of the male capturing the female than courting her.

▶ **The male and female reproductive systems of the Spiny (Piked) Dogfish.**

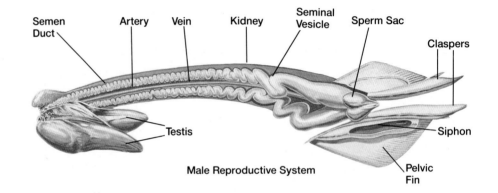

Semen Duct · Artery · Vein · Kidney · Seminal Vesicle · Sperm Sac · Claspers · Testis · Siphon · Pelvic Fin

Male Reproductive System

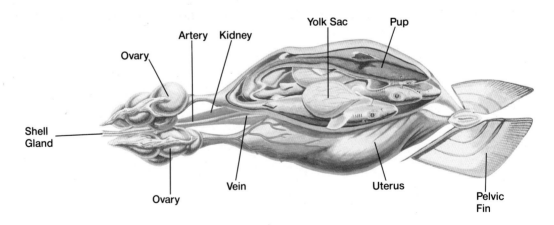

Ovary · Artery · Kidney · Yolk Sac · Pup · Shell Gland · Ovary · Vein · Uterus · Pelvic Fin

Female Reproductive System

By Doug Perrine

How do sharks mate?

In some species, male sharks chase and nip females to presuade them to mate. Some females have skin that is twice as thick as the males'. It protects them during this rough courtship. Before the actual mating can take place, the male must anchor his body. He usually holds onto the female's pectoral fin with his mouth. Only then can he insert one of his claspers in the female's cloaca and release sperm cells into it. (The cloaca is the opening through which wastes are eliminated and baby sharks are born.)

▲This female Tiger Shark has a mating scar on the upper rear portion of her body. These injuries are usually minor scrapes or just nips, but they can cause permanent scars.

Where do sharks mate?

The few matings that have been witnessed took place on the ocean or aquarium floor. Lemon Sharks have been seen mating while swimming belly to belly. Nobody knows where every species of shark mates.

Do sharks mate all year round?

No, there is a mating season, but scientists are unsure when it is for most sharks. They think it may depend on the temperature of the water. Other factors may be involved, too. The Weasel Shark is reported to have two broods per year. Most species have only one.

▶ **The Caribbean Reef Shark is known to mate only once a year.**

By Doug Perrine

How long are female sharks pregnant?

For many live-bearing sharks, this period lasts from nine to 12 months. The Spiny Dogfish holds the record of 22 months—the longest of any shark, and twice as long as the largest whales. Egg-laying species, like the Swell Shark, may be pregnant for just six months before laying their eggs.

Do baby sharks have a special name?

Baby sharks are known as "pups." Before a pup is born, it is called an embryo.

By Doug Perrin

▲ This female Bonnethead Shark was caught on a fishhook. When she was cut open later on, she had this litter of pups inside her.

57

By Doug Perrine

◄This newborn Lemon Shark is still attached to its umbilical cord. The cord must be broken before the pup can swim away.

How are shark pups born?

Shark pups are born in three different ways.

1. As an egg. The embryo develops in a tough egg case. It lives off a rich yolk for up to a year before it hatches. Then it is a fully developed mini-version of its parents. Horn Sharks and Catsharks are egg layers.

2. Born live, with an umbilical cord that connects them to the inside of their mother's body. Hammerhead Sharks, Lemon Sharks and Blue Sharks feed their pups in this way.

3. Born live, without an umbilical cord. Most species feed their embryos in a yolk sac inside the mother's body. The embryo swims around, absorbing the yolk through blood vessels that lead into its body. In some species, the embryo uses up its yolk sac before it's ready for birth. If that happens, it begins to eat unfertilized eggs—or its younger brothers and sisters! Most shark species live in a yolk sac before they're born.

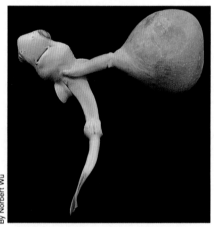
By Norbert Wu

▲This Dogfish embryo is connected to its yolk sac, which will keep it nourished until it is born.

58

How many pups do sharks have?

Grey Nurse Sharks have only two pups. Tiger Sharks give birth to between 10 and 80 pups. Hammerhead Sharks may have as many as 100 in a litter!

▼Leopard Sharks have up to 20 brothers and sisters at a time.

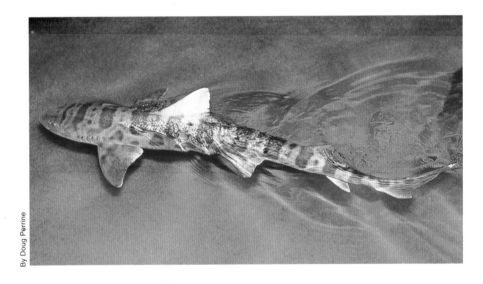

By Doug Perrine

By Wesley R. Strong

◄ Like many shark species, this adult Blue looks very similar to its offspring, only bigger.

How big are newborn shark pups?

Probably the smallest pups belong to the Dwarf Shark. Since it reaches a length of only 9.8 inches (25cm) when it grows up, you can imagine that the pups are quite small! Blue Shark pups are about 20 inches (51cm), and Tiger Shark pups measure about 24 inches (60cm).

How do shark parents take care of their young?

They don't. Shark pups are on their own from the moment they are born. The mother shark does not eat for a while after giving birth, which is good since otherwise she might accidentally eat her own babies! As for male sharks, their parenting ends right after mating!

59

Does a mother shark ever help her pups?

No, though some egg-laying sharks do fasten their egg cases to crags in reef rocks or to the ocean floor so that they don't drift away. But the mother is not around when the pups hatch up to a year later. The eggs are left on their own. Sharks who give live birth don't stay with the pups either.

By Mark Conlin

By Mark Conlin

▲These Swell Shark pups have emerged from their egg cases and have to survive on their own.

▼The Lemon Shark gives live birth to its pups, tail first.

▲Female Horn Sharks often attach their egg cases to the bottom of the sea floor, where the embryos will develop until they are born.

By Doug Perrine

60

What do shark pups eat?

It depends on the species, but most feed on small fish and shrimp.

How long does it take for shark pups to grow up?

Some species grow faster than others. A lot depends on the species, the water temperature and the food supply. Generally, sharks that live longer grow more slowly and mature later than others. Scientists consider a shark mature when it can reproduce.

How do shark pups stay alive?

During their first months of life, some shark pups hide at the bottom of the sea among rocks and ocean reefs. They stay away from animals that could be dangerous to them. Bull Shark pups stay and feed in the shallow lagoons where they were born.

▲These Lemon Shark pups shelter in shallow water in the roots of mangrove trees and seagrass beds.

▼This baby Catshark is resting in its egg case.

61

This young Oceanic Whitetip Shark is being "walked" by a shark scientist. Sometimes when sharks are captured or released, they go into shock and stop swimming. They have to be walked to keep water flowing over their gills. Otherwise, they will die.

SHARKS AND PEOPLE

Our relationship with sharks has depended more on how we think about them than on the nature of the sharks themselves. People have viewed them as pests, as cold-blooded killers and even as gods. The shark's reputation as a man-eater has bred a great deal of fear. Actually, there are many more shark-eating people than people-eating sharks.

Why do sharks attack people?

Sharks attack when they are hungry or when they're afraid. They also attack because, to them, humans swimming sound just like injured fish. Sharks feed on injured fish because they are easy to catch.

▼ **Many people think the Great White Shark is one of the most dangerous creatures in the world. Some cultures, however, treat it as a god and protector.**

Do sharks kill people?

In most cases, shark attacks cause serious injuries, not death. Many deaths are due to blood loss from an initial bite, rather than from repeated attacks.

By Doug Perrine

▲ **The Tiger Shark is large and has been blamed for a number of attacks on humans that proved fatal.**

By Wesley R. Strong

By James D. Watt

Do sharks eat people?

Sometimes, but the majority of shark bites are taste tests. Although the bite may be serious or even fatal, the shark may swim away without feeding. This is because humans do not taste like normal shark food, such as fish or sea lions.

◄ **Although it happens rarely, the Great Hammerhead Shark has been known to attack both people and boats.**

▲ **The Silvertip Reef Shark is a common species. It is large and aggressive and may be a threat to humans.**

► **Not to be confused with the Tiger Shark, the Sand Tiger Shark is not usually considered harmful to humans.**

Do all sharks attack people?

Of the 360-plus species of sharks, only nine are known man-eaters: The Great White, the Mako, the Tiger, the Bull, the Great Hammerhead, the Dusky, the Oceanic Whitetip, the Blue and the Lemon Shark.

Other species have the equipment to attack, but shy away from humans. Some dangerous species live in waters that are too cold or remote to come into much contact with people.

Where do most shark attacks take place?

Most attacks occur where water temperatures range between 68° and 86° F (20° to 30° C). That's mostly—but not entirely—in tropical waters.

▶ **The Great White Shark has attacked humans in both shallow and deep water.**

Is it true that sharks will not attack in shallow water?

No! The majority of attacks occur where people swim—within 200 feet (60m) of the beach and at a depth of five feet (1.5m) or less of water. There are even cases where sharks have beached themselves in attacks on humans!

▲ **The Caribbean Reef Shark is often seen in shallow water and has attacked humans.**

Are any sharks safe to approach?

Not really. If you play with so-called "harmless" sharks or interrupt their normal routines, you are likely to end up with a nasty bite.

Are sharks afraid of humans?

We don't know whether fishes feel human emotions such as fear. Most shark species are not interested in humans and shy away when people approach. On the other hand, some species are attracted to the sounds and smells of humans in the water.

By Doug Perrine

How can I avoid a shark?

Never dive or swim alone or at night. Don't keep captured fish around you in the water. Do not spear fish in the same water over a long period of time. Do not enter the water if you are bleeding. If you see a shark, do not panic or splash around. Get to shore as quickly and quietly as possible.

▲ The Silky Shark is curious and persistent. It will often investigate divers by bumping into them. Reaching 10 feet (3m) or more in length, it is considered potentially dangerous to humans.

Why do people kill sharks?

Humans hunt sharks for their meat and use their skins for leather. The oil found in the shark's liver is used in medicine. Sharks' teeth are used in jewelry and ornaments. And in addition, many sharks are killed senselessly in fishing nets or for sport.

◄These boots were made from sharkskin.

By Doug Perrine

By Doug Perrine

▲This beautiful Tiger Shark was killed just for sport. It was not used for food or anything else.

◄These sport fishermen are going after sharks. Sharks are often killed and stuffed as trophies.

By Doug Perrine

67

Are sharks used in medicine?

Yes. Sharks seem to be resistant to cancer. Researchers are trying to figure out what causes that immunity so that they can use it to treat human cancer. They are working with shark cartilage to find clues to help solve the mystery.

By Doug Perrine

▼Vitamin-rich oil from the liver of some sharks was once widely used for its Vitamin A. Man-made vitamins have ended the need for shark oil.

Do people really eat sharks?

People consume millions of pounds of shark meat each year. Shark dishes are very common in the Far East. Shark fin soup is a great delicacy in Chinese communities. Thresher sharks and Mako can be found in many restaurants and supermarkets. The Porbeagle, a relative of the Great White, is in high demand in Europe. And if you have ever had fish and chips in England, it is possible that you were eating Spiny Dogfish.

▶These sharks were caught for food. Since the heads are inedible, they are discarded. If these sharks had been caught by souvenir hunters, only the jaws would have been taken, and the rest of the animal would have been discarded.

By Wesley R. Strong

68

By Doug Perrine

▲Sharkfin soup is a popular delicacy in China.

▼Sharks' fins are dried out to make sharkfin soup.

By Mark Conlin

What is the shark's place in nature?

The shark is the top predator in the food chain. Without sharks, the world's oceans could become overrun with animals. This would burden sea plants at the bottom of the food chain. These plants create one half of the planet's oxygen. A smaller number of sea plants means less oxygen, and less oxygen means that a smaller number of animals would survive.

What can I do to protect sharks?

Learn more about them. This way you will be able to spread the word that sharks do not terrorize humans, and that randomly killing them is a threat to the environment. There are laws that limit the numbers of some sharks that can be caught, but these limits are often too high or are ignored. You can help work to enact and enforce such laws.

SHARK SPECIES

By James D. Watt

By Doug Perrine

▲This Zebra Shark is a close relative of the Whale Shark, although it is much smaller and colored differently. Both have ridges on their backs and similar mouths.

What is a shark family and what is a species of shark?

A family is a group of living things that share the same characteristics. A genus is a type of animal within a family. Within each genus is one or more species.

How do scientists classify sharks?

The easiest way to show this is to classify one. Let's take a look at the Scalloped Hammerhead Shark.

▲The Latin name of the Scalloped Hammerhead shark classified here is *Sphyrna lewini*. *Sphyrna* means "scoop-head" or "hammer-head." *Lewini* is from the name of the scientist who first described the species.

Kingdom:	Animalia	(animals)
Phylum:	Chordata	(vertebrates)
Class:	Chondrichthyes	(fishes with cartilage jaws)
Subclass:	Elasmobranchii	(sharks and rays)
Order:	Carcharhiniformes	(ground sharks)
Family:	Sphyrnidae	(all Hammerhead sharks)
Genus:	*Sphyrna*	(Hammerheads, Bonnetheads)
Species:	*lewini*	(Scalloped Hammerhead)

How are sharks named?

The person who discovers a new species of shark gets to name it. The name is usually either Latin or Greek. Each species has a first name and a last name. The first name is the genus and the second is its species name. The name describes the shark, the place where it was discovered, or even the name of the person who discovered it.

The Sixgill Shark

One of the most primitive species of shark in the world, these sharks are found mainly in deep water. They have six pairs of gills and gill slits instead of the usual five.

▼ **The Port Jackson shark is named after the place where it was first found, Port Jackson, Australia.**

By Doug Perrine

By David B. Fleetham

▲ **This Sixgill Shark is in the same family as the Sevengill Shark. They look very similar.**

The Nurse Shark

This sluggish shark looks ferocious, but unless you stepped on it in shallow waters, it would probably leave you alone. Its favorite foods are squid, crabs, shrimp, fish and lobsters.

By Doug Perrine

▲ **Nurse Sharks swim along the ocean floor and are slow and awkward. They grow to about 10 feet (3m) long.**

By Doug Perrine

The Wobbegong

With its flat head and round body, and many pieces of skin that look like whiskers, the Wobbegong appears to be a blob of flesh that splashed out and spilled on the ocean floor. Its colors are yellowish brown or grey with spots and stripes.

By Norbert Wu

The Whale Shark

The largest living fish, the Whale Shark is gentle and harmless, living entirely on plankton, shrimp, squid and small fish. It can weigh up to 15 tons!

▶**Whales and dolphins are often seen with scoop-like wounds inflicted by Cookie Cutter Sharks. These bites are probably painful, but not fatal to their victims.**

72

◀**Sailors have mistaken larger Whale Sharks for coral reefs because of their markings—they have whitish spots and stripes on their backs—and slow movements.**

▲**The spotted Wobbegong blends in with the sea floor, where it may spend hours motionless, waiting for its food to pass by.**

The Cookie Cutter Shark

This tropical shark swims up to its victim, usually a whale or large fish, sinks its teeth in, twists its head and escapes with a cookie-cutter-like chunk of flesh. Small, growing only to 20 inches (50cm), it lives in total darkness most of the time, glowing in the dark to attract its prey.

By Norbert Wu

Chain Catshark

This little beauty is named for its dark brown markings that look like chains. Its cat-like eyes are bright green. It is a bottom-dweller in the Caribbean, the Gulf of Mexico and along the east coast of the U.S. It measures only 18 inches (46cm).

By Norbert Wu

By Mark Conlin

▲The Leopard Shark has bold markings, but it is a timid animal.

The Leopard Shark

Some say the most beautiful sharks are the Leopard Sharks. Their bodies have distinctive black saddles and spots on a silvery grey background. They grow to a length of five feet (1.5m).

The School Shark

Also called the "Soupfin" because Asian cultures use its fins to make soup, the School Shark is often captured and killed and may become an endangered species. It measures about 6.5 foot (2m). These sharks may have as many as 50 pups at one time.

▲This beautifully marked shark is known as a Chain Dogfish, but it is actually a Catshark.

▼ Living in shallow tropical waters, the Zebra Shark is often found resting or prowling on the ocean bottom.

By Doug Perrine

73

The Hammerhead Shark

Some scientists believe that this shark's hammer-shaped head helps it find prey because it can sweep a wider area and pick up more scent trails and electrical currents. Its eyes and nostrils are located on either side of its head. Larger Hammerheads may grow up to 15 feet (4.5m).

By Mark Conlin

▲Most large shark species do not travel in schools, but Hammerheads are an exception. These Scalloped Hammerhead Sharks can be a threat to divers.

By Doug Perrine

▲The Whitetip Reef Shark is found in coral coves, reefs and lagoons in the Indo-Pacific Ocean and Red Sea.

▶The Blacktip Reef Shark may swim in small groups throughout its range. It is a common sight in the waters of the Bahamas.

The Whitetip Reef Shark

This shark's name comes from its white-tipped fins. Usually timid, the Whitetip Reef Shark may attack humans when it gets excited. This shark will grow to about six feet (1.8m). Its favorite foods are reef fish, octopuses, crabs and lobsters.

By Wesley R. Strong

By Wesley R. Strong

▲Divers meet up with many species of Reef Sharks along coastal reefs in the Bahamas. They are instructed to use caution when swimming with these sharks.

The Silky Shark

This slender shark is named for its skin, which is smoother than that of most sharks. This is because its denticles are tiny. It can grow to ten feet (3m) or more in length.

▶**Because it is both curious and bold, the Silky Shark is considered dangerous to humans.**

By Doug Perrine

By Doug Perrine

▲**The Bull Shark feeds on other sharks, rays and bony fishes. It can grow up to 11 feet (3.3m).**

▶**The Bull Shark has probably attacked more people than any other species, because it inhabits shallow waters where people swim.**

The Bull Shark

This is one of a small number of shark and ray species that can live in either fresh or salt water. Large, with a heavy body, the Bull Shark travels in warm ocean waters and visits many lakes and rivers around the world.

By Doug Perrine

By Doug Perrine

▲Because they will swallow almost anything, including paint cans and shoes, Tigers have been called "Garbage Can Sharks." In captivity, though, they don't always eat, and usually die if not set free.

The Tiger Shark

Tiger shark pups are born with dark grey spots that fuse into stripes and then fade as the animals mature. Adult Tigers are sometimes longer than 18 feet (5.5m) and weigh over 1,700 pounds (773kg).

By Doug Perrine

▲At certain times of the year, the Tiger Shark swims to shallow waters to feed. It is responsible for many attacks on humans.

The Blue Shark

Known for its bright, metallic blue color and sleek, slinky swimming style, this beautiful shark can reach a length of 13 feet (4m). It is considered dangerous, but it has attacked humans only when it is excited or provoked.

▼The Blue Shark has been known to eat dead or dying whales, but most of its diet is made up of squid and fish.

By Michael Nolan

By Doug Perrine

The Lemon Shark

Believe it or not, Lemon Sharks are not yellow. They are brown and turn a "brassy" color only after they are dead. Their bellies are white. Lemon Sharks can reach a length of 11 feet (3.3m). They don't have to swim to breathe as most sharks do, but can rest for short spells on the ocean floor.

The Basking Shark

The second-largest fish in the world, the Basking Shark can grow longer than 30 feet (9m) and weighs well over four tons. Unlike most sharks, it swims in schools, or groups, with other Basking Sharks.

▲The Lemon Shark has been able to survive reasonably well in captivity. That's why it is one of the few large species that has been thoroughly studied by scientists.

The Goblin Shark

This bizarre creature got its name because of its pale, whitish-grey skin. Its most amazing features are its very long, pointed snout and protruding jaws. It is also called the "Elfin Shark." It grows to 12 feet (3.6m) or more.

▼Like the Whale Shark, the Basking Shark feeds by swimming with its mouth open, filtering thousands of gallons of plankton-rich seawater per hour.

By Tom Campbell

By Bruce Rasner

▲First discovered in 1976, the Megamouth belongs to a family all its own. Its Latin name, *Megachasma pelagios*, means "giant mouth of the open sea."

The Megamouth Shark

The name comes from this shark's huge mouth, which it uses to scoop up plankton. Since only six specimens have ever been found, little is known about its range and habits.

▶The Great White Shark is one of the most feared creatures in the sea. An adult White Shark has no natural enemies except other White Sharks and Killer Whales.

The Thresher Shark

You can tell this shark by its tail, which sometimes is as long as its body. The Thresher may use it to round up the fish it eats as well as to defend itself. It may grow up to 18 feet (5.5m) and weigh as much as 1,000 pounds (454kg).

By H.L. Pratt, Jr., NOAA

▲The Thresher Shark is a very popular food source for many cultures around the world. This one was caught by a commercial fisherman for that purpose.

By James D. Watt

The Great White Shark

This large and dangerous shark can measure 20 feet (6m) and weigh over 3,100 pounds (1,400kg). It is only white underneath. Its back and sides are grey or bronze. The Great White lives in temperate and tropical oceans around the world, but it is not very common anywhere.

By John Hoey, NOAA

◄ This Porbeagle was caught accidentally in a fisherman's gill net. It was preserved for scientists to study.

The Porbeagle

Like its close relatives the White Shark and the Mako, this large and lively shark can keep its body temperature several degrees warmer than the water in which it swims. It needs warm muscles in order to chase speedy fishes like the mackerel and tuna. Reaching 10 feet (3m) in length, the Porbeagle has a white patch at the back edge of the dorsal fin.

By Wesley R. Strong

The Shortfin Mako

Muscular and fast, this dangerous shark can swim at speeds of over 30 miles (48km) per hour. The Mako may grow as long as 12 feet (3.6m) and weigh over 1,200 pounds (540g). Its body is deep blue above with a snow-white belly. Like the Porbeagle and the White, the Mako can raise its body temperature a few degrees above that of the water around it.

By H.L. Pratt, Jr., NOAA

◄One of the fastest sharks in the world, the Shortfin Mako is sought by sport fishermen because it is so hard to catch. It will often jump out of the water—sometimes as high as 20 feet (6m).

▲This Mako was found along the beach. Scientists found the cause of death to be pollution in the water.

Acknowledgments

We would like to thank the following people for their time and contributions to this book: Antonio A. Bentivoglio and Ingo H. Gaida at the University of California at Los Angeles; Dr. Thomas Frazzetta of the Department of Ecology, Ethology and Evolution at the University of Illinois; Jack Carr, Evan Ferrion and Mark Kind of the New Jersey State Aquarium; Paul Gregory and the California Fish and Game Department, Marine Division; Dr. and Mrs. Samuel Gruber, and the University of Miami.

Thanks to the following photographers for their extraordinary photos: Wesley R. Strong, Alex Kerstitch, Howard Hall, Doug Perrine and the International Shark Photo File of Innerspace Visions, Inc., James D. Watts, Mark Conlin, Tom Campbell, Norbert Wu, Mike Nolan, David B. Fleetham,

Len Tillim, Mark Strickland, Chris Huss, John Hoey and H.L. Pratt, Jr., of the National Oceans and Atmospheric Administration, US Department of Commerce, and Bruce Rasner for the rare Megamouth photography.

We would like to express special thanks to Bob Purdy, J.D. Stuart, and the staff at the Natural History Museum of Los Angeles County.

A very special thank-you to Alesha Stoops, Arthur Fredenburgh, Corrine Konz, and Debbie Lynne Stone for emotional support. Also special thanks to a great family: Esther Clover, Terrell Fortner, Diane Smith, Mike, Ryan, Carly, and Matthew Stone. Also thanks to Art and Elva Stone, Linda and Sarah Stone, John and Sandy Johnson, Susan Henley, Blaze Einer, and Sheila Anne Barry for making this project a reality.

Index